# THE THEATERS OF WORLD WAR II
## EUROPE AND THE PACIFIC

### History Book for 12 Year Old | Children's History

**BABY PROFESSOR**
EDUCATION KIDS

World War II, from 1939 to 1945, involved countries in every part of the world. However, most of the fighting took place in Europe and in countries bordering the Pacific Ocean, or on Pacific Islands. Let's look at what happened, and try to understand why.

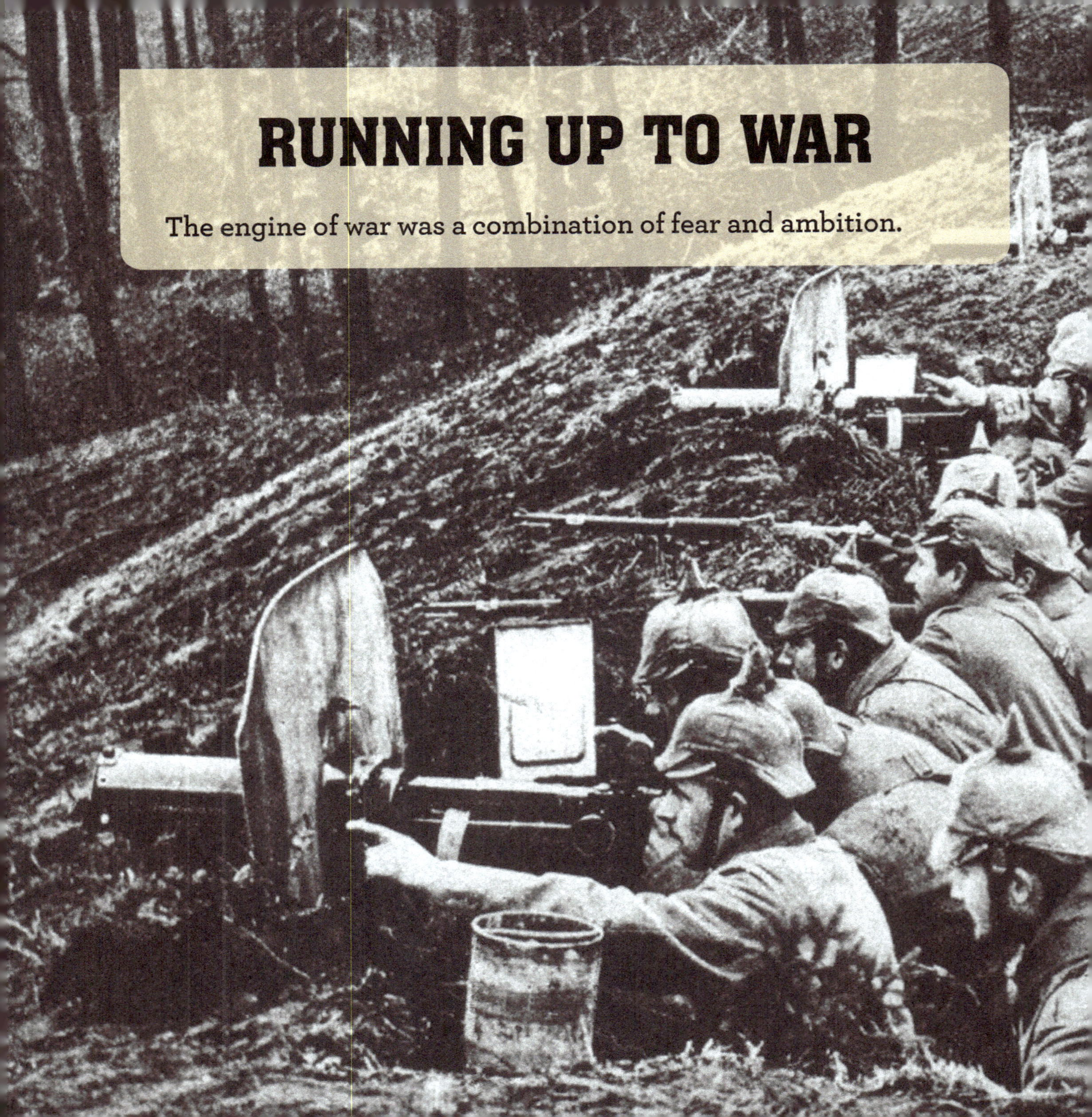

RUNNING UP TO WAR
The engine of war was a combination of fear and ambition.

In Europe, Germany, which had lost World War I (1914-1918), deeply resented the limitations put on it. Under the leadership of Adolf Hitler and the Nazi Party, Germany developed a conviction that it was the "master race" and should be the leading country in Europe, if not the whole world.

Germany pushed and pushed, first to regain the territory it had lost after World War I, and then to impose its will on smaller countries by threat of war. It built a huge war machine that terrified other countries, which wanted to avoid war at all costs. Germany during this time was also fueled by angry words about people trying to undermine the inevitable leadership of Germany. Part of this fury fell on the Jews, who for centuries had been part of German culture and communities. Now, they started being deprived of their businesses, their freedom, and even their lives.

In Asia, Japan had been terrified by two events in the nineteenth century. It watched mighty China fall under control of several European countries, and it found itself not strong enough to resist an American fleet that steamed into Tokyo harbor and demanded that Japan open itself up to world trade.

Japan determined to become a modern world power, to prevent being overrun by the Europeans. It developed a large and efficient army and modernized its resources. It became strong enough to defeat China in a brief war, Russia in another war, and went on to conquer Manchuria and Korea.

Japan decided it either had to conquer eastern Russia (the northern option) or expand into the Philippines, Southeast Asia, and even Australia (the southern option). However, in 1939, Japan lost a badly-handled war with Russia. The high command decided the southern option had a better chance of success.

What happened during the war can be divided into actions in two "theaters". Germany and its allies operated mainly in Europe and North Africa: the European Theater. Japan operated solely in Asia and the Pacific islands: the Pacific Theater.

# 1939-41 EUROPEAN THEATER

In August, 1939, Germany pretended that Poland had attacked Germany. Germany and Russia attacked Poland. Germany expected France, Great Britain, and other countries to talk but do nothing.

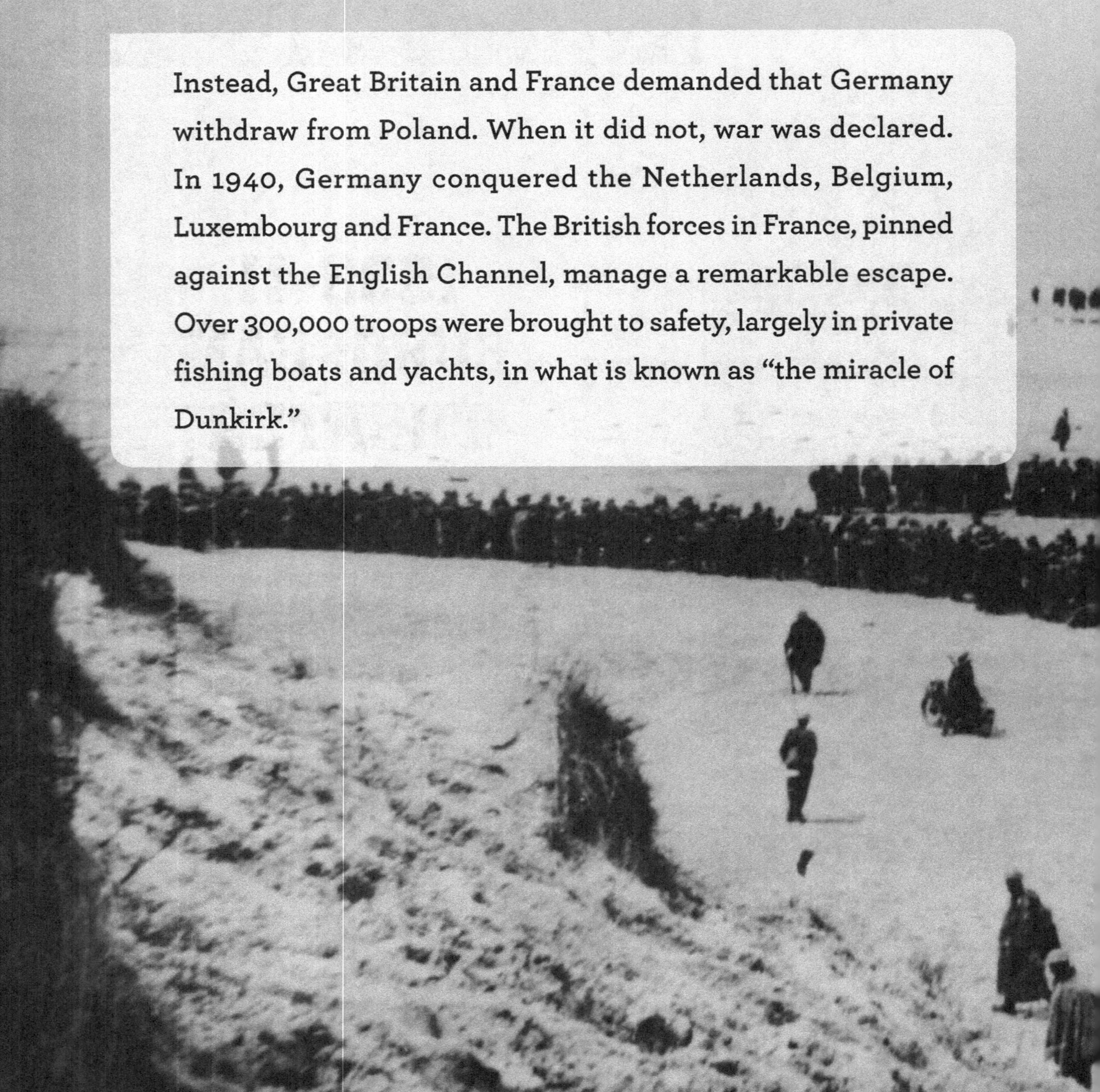

Instead, Great Britain and France demanded that Germany withdraw from Poland. When it did not, war was declared. In 1940, Germany conquered the Netherlands, Belgium, Luxembourg and France. The British forces in France, pinned against the English Channel, manage a remarkable escape. Over 300,000 troops were brought to safety, largely in private fishing boats and yachts, in what is known as "the miracle of Dunkirk."

Italy began an attack against British positions in Egypt, hoping to gain control of all of North Africa and then the Middle East.

By 1941, Italy had not made much progress in southern Europe, so Germany took the lead, conquering Yugoslavia and Greece.

Germany prepared to invade Great Britain, but lost the "Battle of Britain" when the German air force could not defeat the British air force and gain control of the sky.

Instead, Germany launched a surprise invasion of the Soviet Union, which had been its ally until then. Germany drove deeply into Russian territory, hoping to secure oil and gas fields and to knock the Soviets out of the war before turning again to the invasion of the British Isles.

# PACIFIC THEATER

Japan wanted to knock the United States out of the way before continuing its expansion south into the Pacific islands, and to take the Philippines away from American control. It also needed to deal with British possessions like Singapore. So on December 7, 1941 Japan launched a sneak attack on the main U.S. fleet at its base in Honolulu, Hawaii. The attack was a complete success, crippling the fleet; however, instead of suing for peace, the United States declared war on Japan. China and Great Britain followed, and Japan allied itself with Germany and Italy in hopes the three "Axis" countries could conquer the world together.

Japan captured Hong King and invaded Borneo, Malaya, Thailand, many Pacific islands, and the Philippines, while advancing into central China.

# 1942-43 EUROPEAN THEATER

In 1942, as Russia and Germany continued their struggle, the British gained the upper hand against Axis forces in North Africa. They were strengthened when U.S. forces landed in French North Africa, gaining control of Morocco.

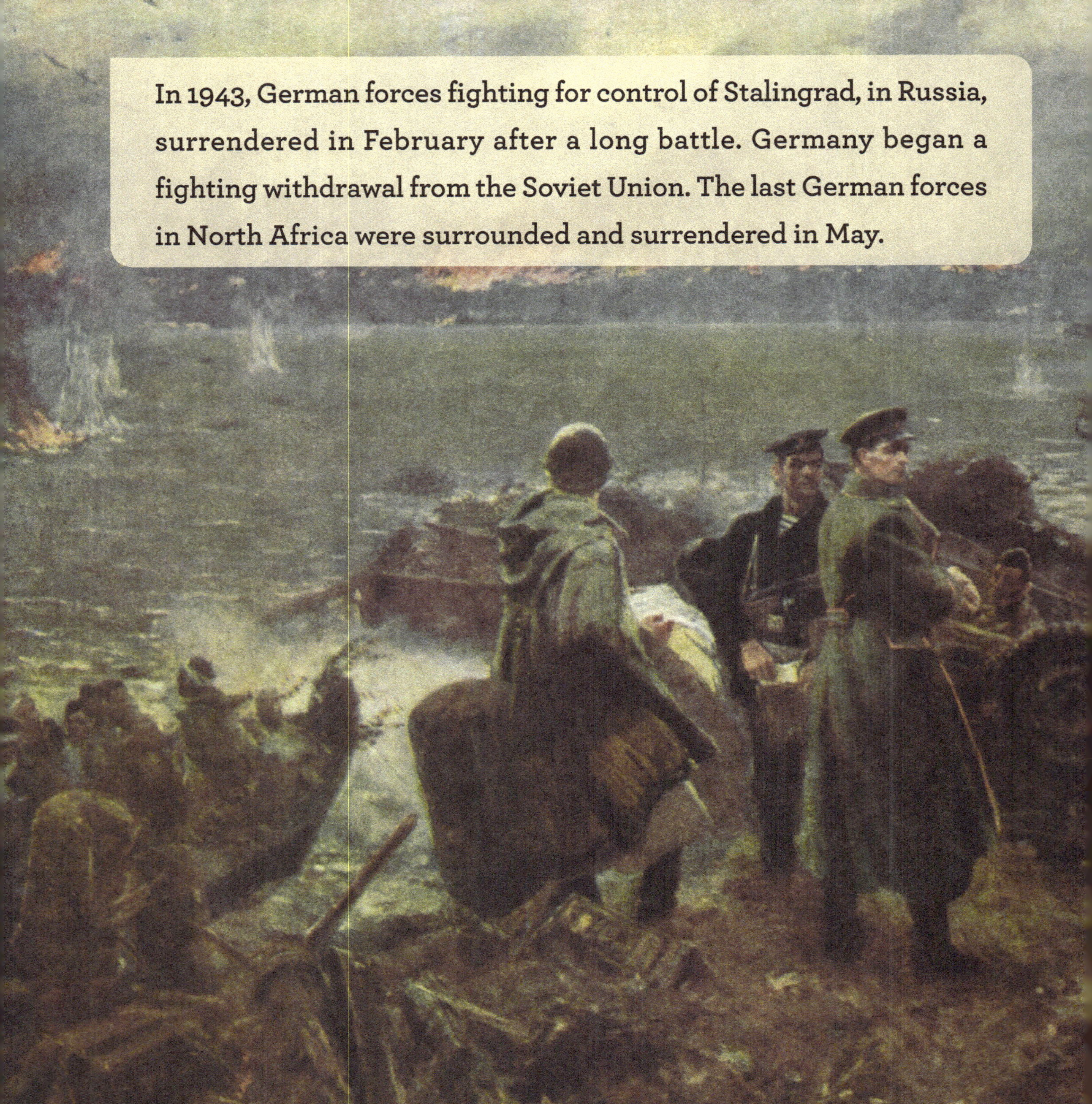
In 1943, German forces fighting for control of Stalingrad, in Russia, surrendered in February after a long battle. Germany began a fighting withdrawal from the Soviet Union. The last German forces in North Africa were surrounded and surrendered in May.

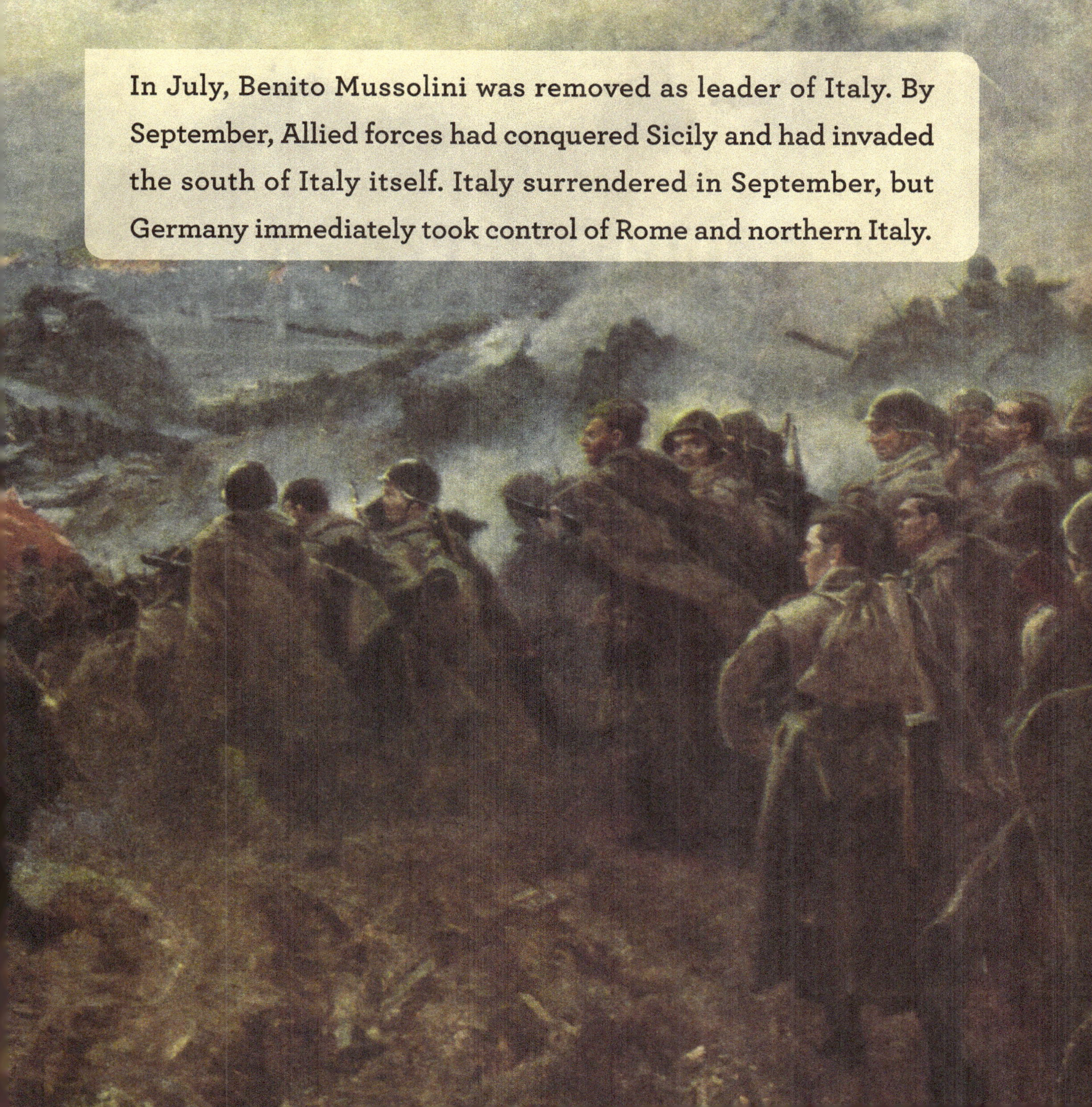
In July, Benito Mussolini was removed as leader of Italy. By September, Allied forces had conquered Sicily and had invaded the south of Italy itself. Italy surrendered in September, but Germany immediately took control of Rome and northern Italy.

# PACIFIC THEATER

In 1942, the British surrendered Singapore, one of their main Pacific territories, to Japan in February. The United States rounded up citizens of Japanese descent on the west coast of the country, and moved them to "relocation camps" on suspicion they might not be loyal. The main U.S. forces in the Philippines surrendered in April and May.

In May and June, Japan lost major naval battles at The Coral Sea and near Midway Island. Many call this the turning point in the war. A great number of Japanese aircraft carriers were sunk and other major ships destroyed. The United States launched the long project of liberating the Pacific islands that Japan had conquered and fortified.

In 1943, the United States continued its island-by-island advance west in the Pacific. At the same time, British and Commonwealth forces brought the Japanese advance through Burma to a halt, and started pushing Japanese forces out of Southeast Asia.

US 1019
US 50
US 1020
US 995

# 1944-45
# EUROPEAN THEATER

In January of 1944, the Allies made a second invasion of Italy, north of Rome. They were able to liberate Rome by June.

As the Soviet Union continued its push on the eastern front, the Allies invaded France in June, landing in Normandy. By August, Paris had been liberated, but fighting continued in eastern France, in Belgium, and in the Netherlands. Athens, Greece was liberated in October.

In 1945, as Germany retreated on every front, the Allies agreed on terms for who would control what after the war was over. This did not always work out well, as you can learn in the Baby Professor book Who Built the Berlin Wall?

In May, Adolf Hitler committed suicide while fighting raged for control of Berlin. Germany surrendered on May 7, and the war in Europe was at an end.

2ND CRUSADE

# PACIFIC THEATER

In 1944, the Allies continued pushing Japanese armies back toward Japan, and retaking Pacific Islands. Fighting raged to liberate Burma and Malaya, and island by island in the Philippines.

Japan at this point was still able to launch offensives in China, pushing deep into Chinese territory and capturing airfields.

By June of 1945, The Philippines and Burma had been liberated, and Chinese forces were advancing against retreating Japanese armies. However, Japan declared it would continue fighting to defend the home islands, and would never surrender.

LITTLE BOY - THE ATOMIC BOMB EXPLODED OVER HIROSHIMA

The allies realized that trying to invade Japan would cost millions of military and civilian deaths. They decided on another route. After giving Japan final warnings, the United States dropped the first atomic bomb used in war, destroying the city of Hiroshima on August 6. As Japan still would not surrender, a second bomb was dropped on Nagasaki three days later.

Within a week, Japan had agreed to surrender. Some isolated forces fought on, but the war in the Pacific Theater was basically over by September 2, 1945.

RUINS OF NAGASAKI, JAPAN

# AFTER THE WAR

Germany and Japan had set out to conquer the world, and failed. The post-war world was instead divided into two major groups, the "West" (although many of its members, like India and Australia, were not in the western hemisphere) with the United States in the lead, and the "Soviet Bloc", nations under the control of the Soviet Union and following communist principles. Learn more about this in the Baby Professor book What is Communism?

To help countries resolve their differences without going to war, a new body, the United Nations, came into existence.

ATIONS UNIES

Those who had led Germany, Italy, and Japan, and who had committed major crimes against humanity, were put on trial for what they had done. Some of those found guilty were executed and others were put in prison. The Baby Professor book What Happens During War Crime Trials? describes this process.

# LEARN MORE ABOUT THE WAR

World War II cost millions of lives and changed the political map of the world. Learn more about it in Baby Professor books like The Allied Powers vs. the Axis Powers in World War II, World War II Brought Advances in Technology, and The Brave Women of World War II.

Visit
BABY PROFESSOR
EDUCATION KIDS
www.BabyProfessorBooks.com
to download Free Baby Professor eBooks
and view our catalog of new and exciting
Children's Books